Early textbooks of English

THE
Polite and Pleaſing
INSTRUCTOR,
OR
ENTERTAINING MUSEUM;
conſiſting of Select

Eſſays, Tales, Fables, Viſions & Allegories,

collected from the moſt

EMINENT ENGLISH AUTHORS:

Prefixed with Rules for

Reading with Elegance and Propriety;

to which is added, a

Collection of Letters and Inſtructions

for Genteel Correſpondence.

LONDON:
Publiſhed Octor. 1ſt. 1783, as the Act directs,
by WILLIAM LANE, Leadenhall-Street.

Title-page of *The polite and pleasing instructor, 1783*

Ian Michael

Early textbooks of English
a guide

Textbook Studies series

Colloquium on Textbooks, Schools and Society

Published by the Colloquium on Textbooks, Schools and Society
© Colloquium on Textbooks, Schools and Society 1993
First published 1993

ISBN 0 9522346 0 2

Printed in the Department of Typography & Graphic Communication
University of Reading

Designed and typeset by Simon Earnshaw, a student in the
Department of Typography & Graphic Communication

Text output in Monotype Sabon, with Arial & Ellington
Printed on Stow Book White Wove 90gsm
Illustration on cover and title-page adapted from a plate in
Joseph Hinchcliffe's *The juvenile speaker* (third edition, 1840)

Distributed by the Reading and Language Information Centre,
University of Reading, Bulmershe Court, Earley, Reading RG6 1HY

This book is designed as an introduction to the history of text-books of English. Three kinds of reader have been kept in mind: those (themselves perhaps collectors of textbooks) who are interested in how the subject used to be taught but cannot pursue it; those who have a general interest in curriculum history; those from other branches of social and educational history such as the development of the book trade, the growth of the professions, and the transmission of knowledge. The selective list of modern works is confined to those which deal with English alone, or with authors in the sample lists. Fuller information about bibliographical and library resources will be given in a similar book introducing research into textbooks generally.

This kind of enquiry is never complete. The compiler will be very glad to hear from those who can supplement or correct the information presented here.

Abbreviations

a.	ante – in or before (a date)
BL	British Library
c.	circa – about (a date)
ESTC	Eighteenth Century Short Title Catalogue
JEGP	Journal of English & Germanic Philology
NLI	National Library of Ireland
NLS	National Library of Scotland
PL	Public Library
RP	Riverside Publications (Microfilm) Woodbridge CT, USA: The Eighteenth Century
UL	University Library

ENGLISH AS A SUBJECT: AN ALLIANCE OF SKILLS

Textbooks of English are difficult to describe. English has always been an alliance of related skills which have been taught, at different historical periods, under various names, in varying combinations and with varying emphasis. In the eighteenth century, for example, a school prospectus could say that the subjects offered included English and grammar: 'English' there meaning only reading and writing. In some sixteenth- and seventeenth-century grammar schools, where no subject called English was taught, translation out of Latin could include careful and specific attention to expression in English, and in the same schools the study of rhetoric could include the reading and imitation of English poetry and the writing of English verse. In the middle of the twentieth century 'comprehension' was treated as a branch of English in the sense that textbooks were issued containing nothing but 'exercises in comprehension'. But comprehension was not a new skill. It was receiving a temporary prominence: students had always (or nearly always) been taught to understand what they read. Why comprehension should be given such prominence at that time is just the kind of question on which the historical study of textbooks of English can have a bearing. It is best therefore to begin a study of textbooks of English with the component skills of the subject, and then to look at the variety of books used in the teaching of those skills.

TEXTBOOKS AND TEXTS

There is another reason for beginning with the skills. Some aspects of English teaching – most obviously grammar – have always relied on textbooks. Others, such as the teaching of composition, were less dependent on textbooks, and, except for manuals of letter writing, there are few of them until the middle of the nineteenth century. But the skill of expressing yourself was taught long before there were textbooks of composition. The teaching of literature requires texts, not textbooks. But in the middle of the nineteenth century there was developed a steadily increasing number not only of texts with a commentary (such as had accompanied *Paradise Lost* for many years) but texts with commentary, notes, biographical information and grammatical exercises (cf nos 55 and 59, below). These literary textbooks were the product of an examination system; they had little to do with the essentials of literature teaching, which required, as had always been the case, texts of particular works, selections from particular authors (no. 45) and anthologies of prose and verse (nos 30, 39 etc). Literature had been taught in schools long before there were, in this narrow form, textbooks of literature.

The question 'what is a textbook?' cannot be answered generally. In each subject, and within branches of a subject, the criteria may vary. A plain text of *Julius Caesar*, without introduction or notes, is a text, not a textbook. But an anthology of poetry which also lacked all critical apparatus would be a textbook if it was explicitly or by implication designed 'for the use of schools'. The compiler, by selection, omission, abbreviation, alteration, has put the poems into a pedagogical context which changes their status. Often of course neither the title nor the preface of an anthology will state that it is meant for schools. Author and publisher both wish the book to have the widest possible sales. By designating it 'for schools' they may lose the domestic market; by omitting 'for schools' they may lose the educational market. By saying that a book is 'for home and school use' they may gain, or lose, both. It is often possible to assess the status of an anthology from its preface. If there is no preface the choice of poems will often show the extent to which the compiler has in mind readers of school age.

CHILDREN'S BOOKS AS TEXTBOOKS

In most subjects, from the middle of the eighteenth century, there are many prose works written for children which are instructional but designed for use at home by a mother or governess. Typical of these are *Histories for youth, being a collection of entertaining stories*, 1740, and *Henry and Edward, or familiar conversations on the elements of science*, 1828. There are similar books on geography, natural science and astronomy. The corresponding books in English are more difficult to identify. Even when fiction is excluded, as in this study, they form a large part of the field of children's literature, and include many works which could have been used in school. We do not however know enough about the details of schooling, in the eighteenth century especially, to say with confidence what kind of prose children's books might have been read before the appearance of class readers early in the nineteenth century. Before then there had been many collections of poetry designed for school (nos 32, 33, 34) and some miscellanies containing verse and prose; but we do not know whether, for example, the younger children attending a well-established private school in 1780 might bring a story book of their own for reading silently; we do not know whether works 'for children' would be in a school library, and if so whether they might be incorporated into formal work. To exclude all children's literature from the category of textbooks would simplify the historian's work but would also distort it. We must judge each such book by the impression it gives. Its cost; the style of its binding; the number of its illustrations; the tone of title and of preface; the way in which the substance of the book is presented, can all help to place it. The decision is difficult, and more than just a refinement of classification. Underlying it is the question whether, and how, literature was taught before it was institutionalized by public examinations, and especially during the second half of the eighteenth century when the interpretative aspects of traditional rhetoric had been flattened into *belles lettres*. Much was written for children at that time. Did it get into the classroom?

It would be possible to step around the status of children's literature by defining a textbook more narrowly: as a manual of explicit, systematic and progressive instruction. Other books, however regularly they were used in school, would then be classed as school books. Such a distinction may be appropriate in some subjects but it would not suit English. It would prejudge important questions about the educational value attached in the past to literature. A verse anthology without commentary could no longer be treated as a textbook. By implication we would be saying that instruction, as a process, and knowledge, as a product, admittedly dominant in educational practice, had been even more powerful than we had supposed, and that the part played by literary and aesthetic experience had been less powerful. There is not enough evidence, in relation to the teaching of English, to support such a view.

THE SKILLS

Textbooks of English are here discussed in relation to four areas
in which it is useful to suppose the exercise of distinctive skills:

1   Reading, spelling and pronunciation (RSP). See p. 13
2   Reading and literature (RL). See p. 21
3   Expression and performance (EX). See p. 31
4   Grammar and language (G). See p. 37

THE PHASES

The historical development of the textbooks, both in numbers
and in content, is complex. It is however possible to see when
some of the most important changes took place, and it is con-
venient to make from these times of change a chronological
framework displaying the development of the books. This
development, up until about 1870, occurred in four phases.

Phase 1   1530–1700
The earliest English rhetorics and spelling books began to appear
during the second half of the sixteenth century. What it is reason-
able to call the first textbook of English (no. 1) was published
about 1532. But few English textbooks were published during
the next 170 years: between 170 and 180 in all.

Phase 2   1701–60
At the end of the seventeenth century there were important
changes. The contents of spelling books now included secular as
well as doctrinal reading matter (no. 6). Some authors of school
grammars began to reinforce contemporary complaints that Latin
grammar (which was supposed to be their model) could not be
comprehensively applied to English, and their textbooks tried to
introduce reform (no. 74). During the early years of the eighteenth
century appeared the first literary anthologies designed for school
use (nos 30, 31, 32). But the number of English textbooks, of all
kinds, was still small: an average of three new ones every year.

Phase 3   1761–1830
The social and economic changes of the second half of the eighteenth century led to an enormous increase in demand for English textbooks. The 1760s mark the beginning of a great change, not in the content of the books but in their quantity. The content changed slowly, responding to a gradual widening of educational demand, but much of the flavour remained the same. It is the quantitative development which is striking. During these seventy years an average of seventeen new English textbooks were produced each year.

Phase 4   1831–70
The 1830s mark a change in the content of many types of textbook. The developments in society which had been taking place during the previous decades were now being reflected in the content of the books. National and church organisations were promoting textbooks in graded series; public examinations were beginning; education was a matter of wider, and more publicized, concern than ever before. The production of textbooks of English doubled at least. On the basis of current figures, which are incomplete, the average annual output of new publications was at least thirty-five. The year 1870 was not of course the end of this process, but it marks another change in many aspects of English teaching; and because we do not yet have the evidence for the years after 1870 which would make it possible to continue the comparison with previous phases it is best to stop the survey at this point.

NUMBERS

Seeing how difficult it sometimes is to say whether or not a book is a textbook of English it may seem absurd to ask how many textbooks were published over a period of 350 years. But it would be useful to know, especially as for the first time there is growing interest in quantitative information of this kind. Table 1 (overleaf) is an attempt to provide it for each of the four skills, in each of the four phases. The numbers are not exact, but they are better than orders of magnitude. They are not estimates. They represent books which exist or are known to have existed. Table 2 presents the same information in the form of the average number of new books published each year. In both tables it is important to remember that the numbers refer to new works, ie. only to the first appearance of a book, excluding all later printings, and that the four phases are of unequal length.

Table 1

Numbers of new textbooks of English, by phase and skill, 1530–1870

	1530–1700 170 yrs	1701–60 60 yrs	1761–1830 70 yrs	1831–70 40 yrs	*Total*
RSP	94	82	339	295	810
RL	31	45	377	519	972
Ex	13	13	136	103	265
G	25	42	379	477	923
Total	*163*	*182*	*1231*	*1394*	*2970*

Table 2

Average numbers of new textbooks of English, published each year, by phase and skill, 1530–1870

	1530–1700 170 yrs	1701–60 60 yrs	1761–1830 70 yrs	1831–70 40 yrs
RSP	0.55	1.36	4.84	7.37
RL	0.17	0.75	5.38	12.97
Ex	0.07	0.21	1.94	2.57
G	0.15	0.70	5.41	11.92

LANGUAGE AND LITERATURE

This is not the place to discuss the validity and significance of the figures in table 1, but it is worth noting one surprise. Although it is generally believed that grammar was the dominant part of English teaching until the second half of the nineteenth century, table 1 shows that the number of textbooks for linguistic study (G) was closely paralleled, in every phase, by the number for literary study (RL). These figures for RL however are influenced by necessarily subjective judgments about the status of verse and prose collections not explicitly for school use. Such works have been included in these numbers with caution.

EDITIONS, IMPRESSIONS AND COPIES

The number of works published gives only a part of the picture. Equally important are the number of impressions and the number of copies sold. When the content of the books is being considered the number of editions and the changes made in them are critical for any account of developments in teaching. Such topics are only now beginning to be studied. Their interest, and their difficulty, is increased by the enormous numbers in which some spelling books especially were issued, over perhaps eighty years, in hundreds of so-called editions (often anonymous and undated), printed in various parts of the country with a text often substantially different from the original. Matters of this kind cannot be pursued here but they offer a fruitful field for local research. This is especially true of elementary textbooks which, though they were, as Crabbe says 'Soil'd, tatter'd, worn and thrown in various heaps', can still be found uncatalogued in libraries and unnoticed on provincial bookstalls. Of some no copies have survived; even of popular books entire editions seem to have vanished.

In the sample entries only a few editions after the first are listed, but an indication is given of the total number. The titles of early books are here often shortened. No attempt is made to do more than show whether an edition is in the British Library. Some other locations are given, but not systematically. Modern bibliographies give locations, but it should be remembered that textbooks are not always included in the library catalogues from which such bibliographies are compiled. London should be assumed as the place of publication if no other is given. An author's other publications are not referred to unless they are directly relevant to the work under discussion.

AMBIGUITIES

The term 'adapted' appears in many titles. It does not imply alteration; it means only 'suited for'. The expression 'upon a plan entirely new' is not a reliable sign of innovation. The term 'English' can also be misleading. In the title of grammars even during the eighteenth century it can mean not 'of English' but 'in English'. The distinction is important. Failure to observe it (or to read the grammar itself) has led to John Stockwood's grammar of Latin (*A plaine and easie laying open of the meaning and understanding of the rules of construction in the English Accidence*, 1590) being described in the *New Cambridge bibliography of English literature* (1.2398) as 'the first grammar of the English language'.

SAMPLING THE TEXTBOOKS

As this introductory book can carry only a sample of the known titles – more than 3,000 in all – the following lists have been kept to an arbitrary total of one hundred: about three per cent. The lists provide sample titles representing each of the four skills in each of the four chronological phases. The hundred books comprising the four lists are numbered continuously, but in each list the books are ordered chronologically. This schematic arrangement is artificial but it derives from, and reminds us of, the different kinds of textbook and the rates at which their numbers increased. Table 3 shows the distribution of the hundred sample titles. It would have been neat to have kept the numbers in each of the sixteen sections proportionate to the numbers in the whole body of books, but the difference between the nineteenth century numbers and the early ones is much too great to make this possible. The sample is meant to be representative also in the sense that it contains some well-known works; some that are neither important nor well-known but are significant in their ordinariness. It should also be remembered that the lists cannot represent adequately the large amount of repetitive hackwork produced by commercial rather than by educational considerations.

Table 3
Distribution of the 100 texts in the sample

	1530–1700 170 yrs	1701–60 60 yrs	1761–1830 70 yrs	1831–70 40 yrs	*Total*
RSP	5	5	9	8	27
RL	2	5	10	15	32
EX	2	2	4	5	13
G	2	4	8	14	28
Total	11	16	31	42	100

HORNBOOK, BATTLEDORE AND ABC

For many children until the end of the seventeenth century the hornbook provided the first step in reading. The battledore served the same function until well into the nineteenth century and the pictorial ABC has never been superseded. They must all be noticed although they are not included in these figures. The hornbook was a small wooden bat onto which was fastened a piece of vellum or paper, covered with horn as protection. It showed some or all of: the alphabet in capital and small letters; a few syllables; the numerals in Arabic, and sometimes in Roman, figures; a devotional text such as The Lord's Prayer. Wooden battledores, inscribed in this way, existed side-by-side with hornbooks. They were replaced during the eighteenth century by stout cardboard ones, which were in turn replaced by rectangular pieces of folded cardboard printed on both sides. The extra space made possible a variety of alphabets, in mixed order; more syllables; some simple sentences. These battledores were printed in vast numbers during the nineteenth century and are still reproduced. Hornbooks are rare, but many museums and libraries have examples of cardboard battledores. The standard work about both is Tuer 1896, below.

ALPHABET BOOKS

Until well into this century practically everyone thought that children learnt to read by first being able to name all the letters of the alphabet and to say them in order. There had been important opponents of this view from the seventeenth century onwards, but it prevailed. The alphabet was printed at the beginning of almost all of a child's first reading matter. As in the copy books the alphabet was often given, in capital and small letters, in three typefaces. Sometimes each letter was accompanied by words which it began, and from earliest times by small woodcuts. The words gave place to verses; the illustrations improved, and by the middle of the nineteenth century the pictorial alphabet was a popular and distinctive production. The pleasure which children took in the pictures was meant to encourage them to learn the letters, but the adults took so much pleasure in the children's pleasure that they made themselves partners in the reading and influenced the publishers to develop the gentle sophistication which is characteristic of the best of these pictorial alphabets.

PRIMER, PSALTER, CATECHISM

In the sixteenth and early seventeenth centuries those who were learning to read passed directly from the hornbook and ABC to the doctrinal texts of primer, psalter and catechism. Like the Bible itself the doctrinal and devotional works which the church used for religious instruction were not composed as textbooks of English. They are relevant because they were the earliest English texts to have been studied in an educational setting, and the only English texts which most children met. It is a commonplace that their influence was profound. The books had behind them the

power and authority of the church, of parents, of the state. Even
if children understood little of the subject matter it was presented
to them as being of the greatest importance, and its power was
confirmed by the strength and beauty of the language. Within the
limits set by the Church's instructional intentions and methods
children could have a measure of literary education, narrow but
of the highest quality.

By the middle of the seventeenth century there were developed
intermediate textbooks which gave extended practice in the reading of syllables (even manufactured ones like *poomd, rewnk*) and
one-syllable words. In an extreme case an entire book could be
composed of lists of single words, as many as 15,000, grouped
by the number of syllables and subdivided according to which
syllable was stressed. Towards the end of the seventeenth century,
and for long afterwards, spelling books often took the form of
all-purpose elementary textbooks. Doctrinal and Biblical reading
passages were supplemented by proverbs, fables and rhymes.
Especially common was the listing of words similar in pronunciation but different in spelling (*fane, feign, fain*). Vocabularies of
hard words were frequent as were grammars, advice on punctuation and a list of silent letters (*p*salm, tho*ugh*). Other features
might be penmanship, arithmetic, ways of expressing time, model
letters and simple book-keeping. By the early nineteenth century
such ancillary skills had their own manuals and disappeared from
the spelling books.

Title-page of *The English spelling book improv'd*, Banbury: J. G. Rusher, *c.*1830

READING, SPELLING AND PRONUNCIATION (RSP)

Reading, spelling, pronunciation, because they exclude writing, are not identical with literacy. It can be argued that literacy is not part of the subject English, but a part of, or a pre-requisite for, every subject. Historically however the teaching of reading (what used to be called 'mechanical' reading) cannot be entirely separated from full reading. The further back we look the more true it is that how you learnt to read and what you learnt to read were the simultaneous concerns of the teacher. The same is true of spelling. Learning to read and learning to spell were so closely connected that, in the seventeenth century especially, they were often identified. Even in 1839 Horace Mann could write, 'The process of learning to spell our language is so imperceptibly lost in that of learning to read it, that the two can best be considered together'. Spelling was thought of both as the enumeration in their correct order of the letters of a syllable and as the correct identification of the syllables which composed a word. The syllables were identified according to a number of rules. Once the syllable had been identified the word could be read by building it up syllable by syllable. Spelling and reading were thus both centred on the syllable.

Although many textbooks, in the nineteenth century especially, included 'pronunciation' in their titles we do not really know how far pronunciation was taught in school. Many early spelling books tried to describe the different sounds of each vowel and the 'force' of the consonants. (The force of the letter d was what is left if you take away from the spoken word 'dog' the sounds represented by -og). Spelling lists were sometimes arranged according to vowel sounds. By the middle of the eighteenth century the teaching of socially appropriate, correct, pronunciation had merged with the performance aspect of reading aloud, speech-making and acting.

The teaching of penmanship is not here considered to be part of English. It may seem inconsistent to include spelling while excluding penmanship. But spelling, reading and pronunciation are linguistic activities, and penmanship is not. A few copybooks used among their models fragments of poetry which were sometimes substantial enough to form a rudimentary anthology (no. 35).

1 (1587) [Francis Clement]
   The petie schole with an English orthographie, wherein by rules lately
   prescribed is taught a method to enable both a childe to reade perfectly
   within one moneth, and also the unperfect to write English aright
      1587 (BL); Pepper R. D. (ed.) *Four Tudor Books*, Scholars Facsimiles,
   Gainesville 1966; Scolar Press facsimile, Menston 1967. Title page as
   plate 3 in Alston 4, below. Clement's preface is dated 21 July 1576, and
   it seems likely that the 1587 edition is enlarged from an earlier work,
   now lost.

2 (1596) Edmund Coote, died before 1620, Master of the Grammar
   School, Bury St. Edmonds
   The English Schoole-Maister, teaching all his scholers, of what age
   soever, the most easie, short, and perfect order of distinct reading, and
   true writing our English tongue that hath ever yet been knowne and
   published by any [etc]
      1596 (BL). A delightful and popular work, its 54th edition appearing
   in 1737. Scolar Press facsimile of 1596 edition, 1968. The title page of
   the 1st edition is plate 4 of Alston 4, below.

3 (1640) Simon Daines, 'Schoolemaster of Hintlesham in Suffs.'
   Orthoepia anglicana: or, the first principall part of the English
   grammar: teaching the art of right speaking and pronouncing English
   with certaine exact rules of orthography, and rules of spelling or
   combining of syllables [etc]
      1640 (BL); M. Roesler and R. Brotanek (eds), Halle 1908; Scolar Press
   facsimile edition 1967. Title page reproduced in plate 7 of Alston 6,
   below. Deals mostly with pronunciation; some spelling and letter-writing.

4 (1688) T. Osborn, 'School-master'
   A rational way of teaching. Whereby children, and others, may be
   instructed in true reading, pronouncing and writing of the English
   tongue [etc]
      1688 (Hamburg UL); Scolar Press facsimile edition 1969. Title page
   in Alston 4, below, plate 26. A representative spelling book. He may be
   the same as Thomas Osborn, 'Minister of the Gospel and teacher of a
   private school in Hatton Garden' whose spelling book has not survived.

5 (1700) Richard Browne, 'Master of a private school, St Ann's
Parish, Westminster'
The English school reformed: containing [letters; spelling lists;
homophones; homographs; numerals; accidence]
  1700 (BL). Ten further editions to 1736; Scolar Press facsimile of
1700 edition, 1969. The title page and another are reproduced as plate
33 in Alston 4, below. Browne's book follows his *English Examiner*,
1692, in spite of the fact that 'many pens have been at work to regulate
the teaching of English.'

6 (1712) Willliam Ronksley
The child's weeks-work: or, a little book, so nicely suited to the genius
and capacity of a little child, both for matter and method, that it will
infallibly allure and lead him on into a way of reading with all ease and
expedition that can be devised
  1712 (BL). An original, relaxed and undogmatic collection of spelling
and reading exercises, verses, riddles, fables and jests.

7 (1719) S. Harland, 'School-master in Norwich'
The English spelling-book revis'd…Part 1 Collected and digested for the
weak apprehensions of children in their first steps to learning. Part 2
Aims at a farther help, when their capacities are grown stronger
  3rd edition 1719 (BL). No copies of the first two editions are known.
His preface discusses the difficulties of teaching reading and spelling.
The title page is reproduced in Alston 4, below, plate 4.

8 (1740) Thomas Dilworth, 'Schoolmaster in Wapping'
A new guide to the English tongue…
  The long descriptive title, about 300 words, is reproduced from the
13th edition (1751), in the Scolar Press facsimile 1967, and in Alston 4,
below. The edition of 1751 (BL) is the earliest to have survived
complete. More than 130 editions of this popular spelling book were
issued – probably many more. Most libraries have copies of some
editions. The work was popular, one supposes, because it contains a
little of everything.

9 (1742) *The child's new play-thing: being a spelling-book intended*
to make the learning to read a diversion instead of a task. Consisting
of Scripture-histories, fables, stories, moral and religious precepts,
proverbs, songs, riddles, dialogues, &c…Divided into lessons of
one, two, three, and four syllables; with entertaining pictures to
each story and fable
  2nd edition 1743 (BL). No copy of the 1st edition has survived.
At least eighteen British and American editions to 1819. An
advertisement / title page is reproduced in Alston 4, below, plate 54.

10   (*a*.1754) Francis Fox, 1675–1738, vicar of St Mary's, Reading
*An introduction to spelling and reading. Containing lessons for children
historical and practical; adorned with sculptures. Together with the
chief rules for spelling, and dividing words into syllables*
     Title from 7th edition 1754 (BL). At least twenty-one editions to 1818
(Bodley). Title page as plate 58 in Alston 4, below. The preface describes
in detail how the book should be used. The tone is sombre. He accepts
the view that children should not be kept to reading the Bible only: his
list of twenty additional books is well represented by '*An Address to
Absentees from the Publick Worship of God, with answers to their pleas*'.

11   (1763) Ann Fisher, 1719–1778, teacher
*The new English tutor: or, modern preceptor. Consisting of orthography
(or the art of spelling and reading) digested into a practical system,
under a few plain easy rules, which any child must be capable of
retaining...Also a practical abstract of English grammar. This work
is beautified with elegant cuts, representing such vices as children are
most addicted to, and such virtues as should be first inculcated*
     3rd edition Newcastle 1774 (Wisconsin UL). No copies of the 1st
edition (1763) or of the 2nd have survived. There are many changes in
subsequent editions, at least fifteen to 1821 (Hull UL). Alston 4. 698,
below, and title page as plate 67. Cf no. 34 below.

12   (1772) John Clarke, 'of Grantham'
*The rational spelling book, or, an easy method of initiating youth into
the rudiments of the English tongue*
     [1772?] (Yale UL). There were at least nineteen editions to 1809, but
few copies have survived. The title page of the 1st edition is reproduced
in Alston 4, below, plate 77.

13   (1781) John Sharp, 'Teacher of the Free English School of Berwick
upon Tweed'
A most easy guide to reading and spelling English, for the use of schools
     Berwick 1781 (BL). The title page is reproduced in Alston 4, below,
plate 82. Sharp prides himself on having arranged his material not by
the number of syllables but by increasing difficulty: '*understanding* is
easier to read or spell than *eye, laugh* or *reign*'. Cf no. 14 below.

14   (1790) John Moscrip, 'One of the teachers of the Free English Reading
School, Berwick upon Tweed'
*The easy instructor: or, the only method to make the orthography and
pronunciation of the English language easy*
     Berwick 1790. Price 8*d*. The title page is reproduced as plate 90 in
Alston 4, below. There are some interesting implications in two teachers
in the same school producing spelling books within ten years of each
other. Cf no. 13 above.

15 (1791/2) [J. Cook], 'A father and a teacher'
*The Westminister spelling-book; or, a child's first book, on a new
plan...calculated so as to attract the attention, please the imagination,
and engage the attention of children, while it cheats them into the paths
of learning*
   Vol. 1, 1792 (BL), price one shilling; vol. 2, 1793 (BL). Facsimile of
title page to vol. 1 reproduced in Alston 4, below, plate 93. Lively and
unconventional. He advocates a system of school inspectors; considers
serious and sacred subjects 'very improper for children'; thinks pictures
a distraction; wants children to enjoy their reading and does not consider
'rat-catching, drum-beating, and song-singing' unsuitable subjects.

16 (1800) Isaac Hewetson
*Reading made easy; or, a step in the ladder to learning: whereby, the
young student is led gradually on, from the easiest words, to those of
two or three syllables*
   Penrith [1800?] Friends House, London. The preface is dated 1800;
the title-page is reproduced in Alston 4, below, plate 110. The material
and organisation is conventional, but he has been influenced by the view
that in most books Scripture names are introduced too early – he
(therefore, or nevertheless) has 'Twenty lessons, in words not exceeding
four letters, from the Book of Ecclesiasticus'.

17 (1802) William Fordyce Mavor, 1758–1837, Headmaster, Woodstock
Grammar School
*The English spelling-book, accompanied by a progressive series of easy
and familiar lessons, intended as an introduction to the first essentials of
the English language*
   [1802?] (Illinois UL). There is uncertainty about the date. Very many
editions, in varying forms, many undated: 32nd edition (Hull UL); 136th
edition 1812 (Reading UL); 217th edition (Bodley); 322nd edition 1826
(BL); 441st edition (Cambridge UL); 468th edition 1859 (BL); another
edition 1902. It is not clear what made the book so popular. Mavor
thought the spelling books by Dyche, Dilworth and Fenning were 'vul-
gar', and claimed that his own reading passages 'tread in the steps of a
Barbauld, an Edgeworth, a Trimmer.' (48th edition 1807). Cf no. 40.

18 (1821) *Reading made most easy; consisting of a variety of useful
lessons. Proceeding from the alphabet to words of two letters only:
and from thence to words of three, four, and five letters &c. so
disposed as to draw on learners with the greatest ease and pleasure,
both to themselves and teachers*
   Workington 1821 (BL). A run-of-the-mill-production.

19 (1829) James Campbell, 'Teacher of English, Arbroath Academy'
The child's economic instructor, Part 1
    2nd edition Arbroath 1829 (BL); 25th edition Edinburgh 1852 (BL),
price 1½d. Part 2 – Arbroath 1829 (BL); 20th edition Edinburgh 1852
(BL), price 3d. Part 3 – 16th edition, Edinburgh 1852 (BL), price 10d. In
part 3 Campbell claims that the meanings given to selected words before
each extract are 'a novelty in books of this class.' He also explains that
'a system of mental exercises' (understanding what is read) promotes
progress, as 'bare reading' does not.

20 (1833) *The anti-spelling book; a new system of teaching children to
read without spelling. With an introduction addressed to parents and
teachers*
    1833 (Hull UL; Leeds UL). The 2nd (BL 1568 / 1099), 3rd (BL) and
6th (BL) editions are all dated 1834. BL attributes authorship to René
Aliva. The author's positive recommendation is that reading is learnt
cumulatively.

21 (*a*.1842) Robert Sullivan, 1800–68, 'Inspector of Schools'
*The spelling-book superseded; or, a new and easy method of teaching
the spelling, meaning, pronunciation, and etymology of all the difficult
words in the English language; with exercises on verbal distinctions*
    Title from 23rd edition 1851. 4th edition Dublin 1842 (Bodley); 29th
edition Dublin 1853 (BL); 221st edition 1886 and editions to 1920.
Revisions in 1851 made it almost a new work. The book is based on
types of word – homophones, synonyms – and on derivations. See
below M'Alester 1961.

22 (1851) *The child's treasure: or, reading without spelling, effectually
simplified by a novel system; which is also equally available in the
present mode of teaching to read; and in which are separately taught:
1, The long sounds of the vowels. 2, Their short sounds. 3, Their other
sounds, &c. &c. By a lady*
    1851 (BL). The preface expresses astonishment that there has not yet
been 'a systematic arrangement of the almost insurmountable difficulties
of learning to read'.

23 (1854) *The word-making primer, designed for use in elementary
schools. By a schoolmaster*
    1854 (BL). The author recommends the use of the blackboard (which
he says is a novelty in teaching reading). Syllables and then words are
built up on the board. The book comprises material formed in this way.

24   (1857) Favell Lee Bevan, (after 1841, Mortimer), 1802–78
     Reading without tears; or, a pleasant mode of learning to read
         1857 (BL). Many unnumbered editions to at least 1924. A successor
     to her *Reading disentangled*. She bases her approach on pictures, on the
     grading of material and on the omission of irregular words: 'equally
     well adapted to the new, or to the old system of learning to read'.

25   (1866) Edward N. Marks
     The ear and the eye; or, a new way to try. A picture primer in rhyme
         Edinburgh 1866 (BL). Restricted to a vocabulary of 500 words.

26   (1866) W. H. Unger, 'Assistant master, the Royal School of Armagh'
     A short cut to reading. The child's first book of lessons
         London (Armagh printed) 1866 (BL). It is 'frequent seeing' that
     teaches spelling.

27   (1869) Adolf Sonnenschein, 1825–1913, & John Miller Dow
     Meiklejohn, 1836–1902, Professor of Education, St Andrews
     The English method of teaching to read
         Four parts, 1869 (BL), preceded by *The Nursery Book*. A 'look-
     and-say' approach, highly systematized with instructions to teachers.
     Spelling should be taught 'only by dictation'.

CONTENTS.

BOOK I.   SACRED AND MORAL.

BOOK II.   DIDACTIC, DESCRIPTIVE, NARRATIVE, AND PATHETIC.

The

Vicesimus Knox, *Elegant extracts...of poetry*, (no. 38 below) from an undated edition before 1787

READING AND LITERATURE (RL)

A main purpose of this sample is to illustrate the variety of textbooks which were used in the teaching of literature. The term
'literature' carries here its broadest, and powerfully legitimate,
sense. The enlargement of imaginative experience can come from
Mrs Barbauld's *Lessons for children* and from *Samson Agonistes*.
The need to distinguish between textbook and text is discussed
above. The most straightforward, but not the only, criterion is the
presence of notes or other explanatory matter.

The teachers' attitudes to literature, and what they selected for
their pupils, is a fascinating topic too vast to be considered here.
In the seventeenth century the material chosen for young children
was almost entirely scriptural, doctrinal or devotional. Secular
material became increasingly frequent from the early eighteenth
century, but was heavily moralistic throughout. From the early
nineteenth century class readers included factual selections from
technology, history, geography and natural science. The curriculum of the grammar schools was necessarily classical, but teachers
of rhetoric drew illustrations from the English poets, and English
verse translations of Homer and Virgil were used to an extent we
cannot assess. From the end of the sixteenth century verse
anthologies were popular and there is some evidence that the
publishers expected them to be used in school (no. 28). The main
markets for literary textbooks during the eighteenth century were
home, where most girls were educated, and the private schools
and academies. In the nineteenth century the main influence
(apart from public examinations) on textbooks was the desire to
make English literature as respectable academically as were the
classics. This was to be achieved through extensive linguistic
annotation and solid biographical summaries.

28 (1597) Nicholas Ling, compiler
Politeuphuia: wit's common wealth
    1597 (BL). More than thirty further editions to 1722. One of a
number of anthologies containing aphorisms, epigrams, proverbs, short
verse and prose quotations. By 1699 the title-page had added 'for the
use of schools', and it is likely that the book had already been used as
a stimulus for schoolboys' composition.

29 (1657) Joshua Poole, died before 1657, teacher
*The English Parnassus: or, a helpe to English poesie. Containing a
collection of all rhyming monosyllables, the choicest epithets, and
phrases: with some general forms upon all occasions, subjects, and
theams, alphabetically digested*
    1657 (BL); another edition 1677; 1678. Facsimile edition, Scolar
Press 1972. This extraordinary book is a collection of more than
30,000 epithets and 22,000 quotations, designed to help in the writing
of English verse and acting also as a compressed literary anthology.
Verse writing is the path to literature. The 'general forms' are modes
such as praising, protesting, giving thanks, for which phrases are listed
in a few final pages. Hoole (1660), recommends *The English Parnassus*
for use in the fourth form. See below Wallis 1954.

30 (1717) James Greenwood, died 1737. 'Teacher of a boarding-school at
Woodford, Essex'; later Sur-master of St Paul's School
*The virgin muse. Being a collection of poems from our most celebrated
English poets. Designed for the use of young gentlemen and ladies, at
schools...With notes, and a large index, explaining the difficult places,
and all the hard words*
    1717 (BL); 2nd edition 1722 (BL); 3rd edition 1731. The first book of
its kind. It contains 126 passages, most from Cowley, then Milton and
Dryden; none from Shakespeare. Cf no. 75, below.

31 (1737) John Warden, 'Teacher of English'
*A collection from The Spectator, Tatler, Guardian, Mr Pope, Mr
Dryden, from Mr Rollin's Method of teaching the Belles Lettres,
and his Universal History. For the benefit of English Schools*
    Edinburgh 1737 (Glasgow UL); Newcastle-Upon-Tyne 1752 (Hull UL;
Nottingham UL); Newcastle 1761 (BL), Edinburgh 1765 (BL). The only
comments (in the 1761 edition) are on Homer and Virgil, and these are
appreciative rather than explanatory. There is no preface. See below
Law 1984.

32   (1746) *The art of poetry made easy, and embellish'd with great variety*
     of the most shining epigrams, epitaphs, songs, odes, pastorals, etc from
     the best authors
          London: J. Newbery 1746 (BL); 2nd edition and subsequently as
     Poetry made familiar, 1748 (BL). Five editions in all to 1788. Often
     attributed to John Newbery himself, on insufficient evidence. The title
     pages of the first three editions are reproduced in Roscoe 1973, page 80.
     This simple book is outstanding for the integrity and good judgement
     with which it is compiled and for the clarity of its exposition. 'The
     whole Aim and Intention of Poesy is to please and to instruct'. Its
     emphasis is on pleasure. Cf no. 77, below. See below Noblett 1972;
     Roscoe 1973.

33   (1750) *The Edinburgh entertainer: containing historical and poetical*
     collections. For the use of schools. Taken from the best authors
          Edinburgh 1750 (BL). Contains seventeen prose and thirty verse
     passages. The prose is from either Buchanan's *Scottish History* or
     from classical histories. The verse includes Gay, Parnell, Pope,
     Thomson. No preface or commentary.

34   (1756) [Ann Fisher, 1719–78, teacher]
     The pleasing instructor: or, entertaining moralist. Consisting of select
     essays, relations, visions and allegories, collected from the most eminent
     English authors...Designed for the use of schools...to form the rising
     minds of the youth of both sexes to virtue, and destroy in the bud, those
     vices and frailties, which mankind, and youth in particular, are addicted to
          1756 (BL); about forty further editions to the 1830s. Ann Fisher, who
     ran a girl's school in Newcastle-upon-Tyne, was particularly concerned
     with the education of girls, and wrote several influential textbooks.
     After marrying Thomas Slack she had nine daughters, all of whom
     survived her. The prose passages are almost all from *The Spectator*
     and other periodicals. Cf no. 11, above.

35   (1761) John Tapner, 'Schoolmaster at Boxgrove, in Sussex.'
     The school-master's repository: or, youth's moral preceptor.
     Containing a select store of curious sentences and maxims, in prose
     and verse. Together with the greatest variety of copies in single and
     double-line pieces, hitherto published. Designed more particularly
     for the use of schools
          [1761] (BL). A collection of short pieces, up to six lines, suitable for
     writing copies. The book is designed for 'private country schools'.

36 (1762) *The poetical miscellany; consisting of select pieces from the works of the following poets, viz. Milton, Dryden, Pope [etc] For the use of schools*
   1762 (BL); 2nd edition 1769; 3rd edition 1778 (BL); 4th edition 1789 (BL). 'The editor thinks...that every sensible and unprejudiced Parent will be better pleased to hear his Son repeat fifty lines of Milton, Pope, Young, or Thomson, than five hundred of Ovid or Virgil'. Shakespeare is not represented in the 1st edition but has appeared by the 3rd.

37 (1774) William Enfield, 1741–97, lecturer, Warrington Academy
   The speaker: or, miscellaneous pieces, selected from the best English writers, and disposed under proper heads, with a view to facilitate the improvement of youth in reading and speaking. To which is prefixed an essay on elocution
   1774 (BL; Cambridge UL; Warrington PL). An immensely popular and influential collection which had at least sixty editions and impressions to 1863. Many more passages from Shakespeare than from any other writer.

38 (c.1784) Vicesimus Knox, 1752–1821, headmaster, Tonbridge
   Elegant extracts: or useful and entertaining pieces of poetry, selected for the improvement of youth in speaking, reading, thinking, composing; and in the conduct of life
   [c.1784] (BL). The first two editions were undated. At least sixteen editions to 1826. Knox compiled two companion works: *Elegant extracts...in prose*, 1783 and *Elegant epistles*, 1790. All were popular (the letters less so) and shortened versions of each were published. The full versions, intended for school, but probably not for classroom, use, run to between 700 and 1100 pages. See below Blunden 1963; Goldsmith 1980; Hansen 1987.

39 (1799) Lindley Murray, 1745–1826
   The English reader; or, pieces in prose and poetry, selected from the best writers. Designed to assist young persons to read with propriety and effect...
   York 1799 (BL; Leeds U. Museum of Education). More than thirty editions and impressions to 1860. The pieces, Murray says, are more grave than gay, but other selections are more gay than grave. He stresses 'the necessity...of precisely ascertaining the meaning of what we read'. Shakespeare is excluded. In some pieces Murray has made alterations 'to adapt them better to the design of his work'. Cf no. 84 below.

40   (1801) William Fordyce Mavor, 1758–1837, sometime teacher, and
Samuel Jackson Pratt, 1749–1814, very miscellaneous writer
*Classical English poetry, for the use of schools, and of young persons
in general. Selected from the works of the most favourite of our national
poets*
   1801 (BL). About twenty editions to 1837. Pratt's name was soon
dropped. Epic and dramatic verse are excluded. The poet most
represented in the 1st edition is John Langhorne. Mavor and Pratt
have fourteen poems between them. Cf no. 17 above.

41   (1816) Richard Edgeworth, 1744–1817, and Maria Edgeworth,
1767–1849
Readings on poetry
   1816 (BL; Leicester UL); 2nd edition 1816 (BL; Nottingham UL). A
detailed discussion, for young people, of poems chosen from Enfield's
Speaker. The explanations and the long preface are admirable.

42   (1818) Alexander Jamieson, Wye House Academy, Brentford
*A grammar of rhetoric and polite literature; comprehending the principles
of language and style, the elements of taste and criticism: with rules
for the study of composition and eloquence...for the use of schools, or
private instruction*
   1818 (BL); 2nd British edition 1823 (BL; Nottingham UL); fourteen
American editions to the 1870s. The work deals with poetry, grammar
and composition, and is intended, in part, to bring the teaching of
George Campbell, Blair and Kames nearer to the classroom.

43   (1822) [John Rogers Pitman], 1782–1861, perpetual curate of Bearden
*The school Shakespeare; or, plays and scenes from Shakespeare,
illustrated for the use of schools, with glossarial notes, selected from
the best annotators*
   1822 (BL); 1834 (BL). Comprises Rowe's life of Shakespeare,
Johnson's preface, scenes from nine plays, and twelve sonnets. The
notes explain vocabulary and allusions.

44   (1827) Anna Terminia Riley, Albion House [School?], Epsom
*Analysis of poetry; an attempt to develop the elements of figurative
language, with a view to facilitating the study of poetical criticism.
Intended for the use of schools*
   1827 (BL). A most unusual book, not so much for its contents as for
the hope that it might be used in school. It is a study in psychology,
applied to the teaching of poetry. Its contents include chapters on the
transfer of sensory epithets ('scarlet pain'); transfers by analogy; poetical
invention; the sublime; 'poetical criticism' and 'poetical analysis'. Many
illustrations from poems read in school.

45 (1831) Joseph Hine, teacher, Brixton Lodge, Surrey
*Selections from the poems of William Wordsworth, esq; chiefly for the
use of schools and young persons*
   1831 (BL); two later editions. The book is intended for class use, a
copy for each pupil. Wordsworth visited Hine's school and allowed him
to make the selection because he understood the merit of poems such as
The Idiot Boy.

46 (1831) John Murray McCulloch, Headmaster, Circus-Place School,
Edinburgh
*A series of lessons, in prose and verse, progressively arranged; intended
as an introduction to A Course of Elementary Reading in Science and
Literature. To which is added, a list of prefixes, affixes, and Latin and
Greek primitives*
   Edinburgh 1831 (BL). Fifty-eight editions to 1882. 'Lessons' are
passages to be read. The book claims to be representative of the
class-books 'compiled on more simple and natural principles' than
the 'speakers' that used to be fashionable. He attributes 'bad morality
and false religion' to 'such writers as Shakespeare, Chesterfield and
Hume.' Cf no. 88 below.

47 (1835) Henry Innes 'Professor of elocution, lecturer on rhetoric
and literature'
*The British youth's reader: or, exercises in English history, natural
history, biography, poetry, etc*
   1835 (BL). His principal rule for the 'acquirement of an easy,
graceful, and nervous elocution' is to practice daily for fifteen to
twenty years. The 'exercises' are just the passages themselves.

48 (1835) Meshach Seaman
Select verses of the modern poets, for the use of schools
   Colchester 1835 (BL). The selection is strongly biased towards
religious subject matter and it seems that much of the verse comes
from contemporary journals. James Montgomery is called 'the first
of living poets'.

49 (1838) Gething, Mrs
*Selections from modern authors for the use of the higher classes
in schools*
   Darlington 1838 (BL; Bodley). The usual selections for schools are
spoilt by 'the constant recurrence of the same lessons.' This collection
aims at variety.

50   (1845) Ireland, Commissioners of National Education
Reading book for the use of female schools
     Dublin 1845 (NLI; personal); at least six later editions to 1862. Prose
and verse: the prose partly vocational ('Duties of a cook'), partly general
knowledge and conduct. The verse nearly all nineteenth century. No
commentary. Cf no. 68 below.

51   (1848) John Frederick Boyes, 1811–79, headmaster of Walthamstow
Proprietary School
*English repetitions, in prose and verse, for the use of the senior classes
of schools; with introductory remarks on the cultivation of taste in the
young, through the medium of our own writers*
     1848 (BL). The introductory remarks are a forty-page essay, full of
interest, on contemporary education. Contains 114 passages, from
Shakespeare to Byron.

52   (1849) Walter McLeod, headmaster of the Model School, Royal
Military Asylum, Chelsea
*The first poetical reading book. Compiled for the use of families and
schools. With introductory descriptions and explanatory notes*
     1849 (BL; Cambridge UL). A conventional selection; paraphrase and
memorizing encouraged.

53   (1852) George Frederick Graham
*Studies from the English poets: a reading-book for the higher classes in
schools, or for home teaching*
     1852 (BL). The passages are meant to provide material for 'poetical
criticism', and some are provided with 'examination questions'. Graham
seems to have been a professional writer of textbooks. Cf no. 69 below.

54   (1859) Alexander Winton Buchan, 'Teacher, Glasgow'
*The poetical reader: a new selection of poetry for the school-room, with
notes and questions*
     Edinburgh 1859 (BL); 2nd edition 1861 (BL; NLS). Some extracts are
accompanied by questions, such as (on Coleridge's *Hymn before
Sunrise*) "Explain the expression, 'the soul in her *natural form*'".

55   (1859) John Hunter, vice-principal, Battersea Training College
*Shakespeare's Henry the Eighth. With introductory remarks; copious
interpretation of the text; critical, historical and grammatical notes;
specimens of parsing, analysis, examination questions, etc, and a life of
Cardinal Wolsey*
     1860 (BL); 1872 (BL).

56 (1862) Coventry Patmore, 1823–96
    The child's garland from the best poets
        1862 (BL; Glasgow UL); 1873 (BL); 1883 (BL); 1895. The criterion
    of selection is 'having actually pleased intelligent children...[which]
    test has excluded nearly all verse written expressly for children'.

57 (1863) James Stuart Laurie, 1832–1904, formerly inspector of schools
    Standard series of elementary reading books, 1–6
        Longman 1863 (BL); 1866 (BL). A revision of the *Graduated series*,
    1860–1, which was too expensive for each pupil to have a copy. This
    series is cheaper. The arrangement 'will be found equally applicable to
    the analytic and synthetic methods of teaching reading': teachers who
    have not adopted 'the look-and-say' system should try it.

58 (1863) Edward Thomas Stevens and Charles Hole, headmaster of
    the Loughborough Collegiate School, Brixton
    *The grade lesson books, in six standards. Especially adapted to meet
    the requirements of the 'revised code'*
        Longman 1863; 1871 (BL). Each book quotes, and keeps closely to,
    the skills laid down for that standard.

59 (1870) Thomas Armstrong, headmaster, Heriot School, Edinburgh
    Compendium of English literature for the use of schools and students
        Edinburgh [1870] (BL). Prose, poetry and drama in periods. With
    503 questions and answers and occasional illustrative passages.

37
COMPACT SENTENCES.

WHEN each clause or portion of a sentence is connected in signification with that which has preceded, and the meaning of the speaker or writer cannot be known until the concluding accent of the last word is repeated or read, the *whole* is called a *Compact Sentence.—Example:* 'Having already shewn how the fancy is affected by the works of nature, and afterwards considered in general both the works of nature and of art, how they mutually assist and complete each other, in forming such scenes and prospects, as are most apt to delight the mind of the beholder, I shall now throw together some reflections on that particular art, which has a more immediate tendency than any other to produce those primary pleasures of the imagination which have hitherto been the subject of this discourse.'

A Scale of the principal Inflexions in Compact Sentences.

Is it Á or B̀?

The voice in pronouncing 'A' ascends from the middle of the scale to the top; in pronouncing 'B' it descends from the middle to the bottom: they are called, therefore, the extreme Rising and Falling Inflexions.

'Is it' are two unaccentuated syllables of the former oratorical word ;—('isitá?') 'or' is the unaccentuated syllable of the oratorical word 'orbè.'

Pupils should be taught to pronounce the whole Alphabet in this manner, until the ear be rendered perfectly familiar to both these Inflexions. Is it Á or B̀?—Is it B̀ or Ċ?—Is it Ċ or D̀? &c. &c.

EXPRESSION AND PERFORMANCE (EX)

This group of skills has less need for textbooks than any other. Sixteenth- and seventeenth-century manuals of rhetoric in English were designed to prepare schoolboys for making speeches in public life: in parliament, in the lawcourts and in the pulpit. Written exercises were imitations of classical orators. The quality aimed at was persuasiveness, to be achieved through the skillful handling of the prescribed parts of an oration and of the figures of speech. Outside this framework the only original composition was the writing of verse, also dependent on imitation, which produced pastiche (no. 29). From the middle of the eighteenth century until well into the nineteenth the performance aspects of rhetoric were taught as elocution, and textbooks were published teaching the management of voice and gesture not only in making speeches but in recitation, reading aloud and (to a very limited extent) acting. Written composition took the form of theme and essay (no. 66). There are several published collections of prize verses written by pupils, as well as speeches for special occasions (no. 67). Composition was unpopular with both pupils and teachers. The making of summaries, often of the sermon, had long been a school child's task but the only textbooks the skill generated are the manuals of precis designed to prepare for Civil Service examinations. Manuals of letter writing had existed since the Middle Ages but relied almost entirely on the imitation of model letters.

60 (*c.*1525) Leonard Cox, *c.*1490–1557, poet, master of Reading School
The arte or crafte of rhethoryke
    (Cambridge UL; BL). Another edition 1532 (Bodley); F. I. Carpenter,
    (ed.) Chicago 1899, reissued AMS Press [1975]; facsimile of first edition
    Amsterdam, English Experience, 1977; R. L. Freeman, (ed.) Lanham,
    Md 1986. The rhetoric deals only with expression. It is intended for
    'yonge studientes' and for 'all them that have any thynge to perpose or
    to speke afore any companye what somever they be'. See Breeze 1988.

61 (1672) R. S.
*Ludus ludi literarii: or, school-boys' exercises and divertisements. In
XLVII speeches: some of them Latine, but most English; spoken (and
prepared to be spoken) in a private school about London, at several
breakings up, in the year 1671*
    1672 (BL). There are forty seven speeches, of which six are in Latin.
    R. S. is anxious to encourage the use of English, even though many of
    the subjects are 'as petite, and little as can be thought of.' Topics include
    'Upon a Mince-Pye', 'Upon Boys that can learn, and wont'. His book is,
    he says, 'the first Essay of this nature that ever came in print, or has
    been made by any one.'

62 (1721) Isaac Watts, 1674–1748, private tutor; pastor; hymn writer
*The art of reading and writing English: or, the chief principles and rules
of pronouncing our mother tongue, both in prose and verse; with a
variety of instructions for true-spelling*
    1721 (BL). At least thirty editions of various kinds to 1813. Facsimile
    of 1721 edition, Scolar Press 1972. Mainly about the skill of reading
    aloud; sensible and simple.

63 (1739) John Holmes, b. 1702, master of the Grammar School, Holt
*The art of rhetoric made easy: or, the elements of oratory briefly stated,
and fitted for the practice of the studious youth of Great Britain and
Ireland*
    1739 (BL). Eleven editions to 1849, usually combined with John
    Stirling's *A system of rhetoric*, 1733. A conventional rhetoric, slightly
    idealising practical school work. Part 1, 96 pages, is meant to be learned
    by heart. Part 2 is a summary of Longinus and a list of figures and
    tropes.

64 (1761) [James Burgh] 1714–75, master of an academy at Stoke
Newington
*The art of speaking. In two parts. Containing 1, an essay, in which are
given rules for expressing properly the principal passions and humours,
which occur in reading or publick speaking. 2, Examples of speeches
taken from the antients and moderns*
   1761 (Manchester PL; Glasgow PL); title from second Dublin edition
1763 (BL). Alston 6 (below), pp 334–54, records twenty-two editions in
all to 1804. Burgh thinks 'young persons ought not to be put upon
writing (from their *own funds*, I mean) till they have furnished their
minds with *thoughts*...But they cannot be kept from speaking.'
Interpretation is based on the expression of the passions and emotions
(seventy-six are listed, with passages for practice). Recommended to
Coleridge by his brother Luke.

65 (*c*.1800) *The theatre of youth; being a selection of pleasing dramas, for
the improvement of young persons*
   Huddersfield [printed between 1798 and 1807]. (Bedford College of
Higher Education). Contains three rather stilted and moralistic plays,
which are unusual in having rudimentary stage directions. No indication
of either home or school use.

66 (1801) John Walker, 1732–1807, actor, teacher of elocution
*The teacher's assistant in English composition; or, easy rules for writing
themes and composing exercises, on subjects proper for the improvement
of youth of both sexes at school*
   (Hull UL). Editions from 1805 usually as *English themes and essays;
or, the teacher's assistant*...At least twelve editions to 1853. Walker
wrote twelve books related to English teaching, including the influential
A critical and pronouncing dictionary, 1791.

67 (*a*.1816) Thomas Ewing, 'Teacher of English, geography and history,
Edinburgh'
*Principles of elocution; containing numerous rules, observations and
exercises, on pronunciation, pauses, inflections, accent and emphasis;
also copious extracts in prose and poetry; calculated to assist the
teacher, and to improve the pupil, in reading and recitation*
   Edinburgh 1816 (NLS; BL). According to the preface, dated November
1815, this is a revised edition, in which there are fewer rules and more
extracts. At least thirty-eight editions to 1870.

68 (1837) Ireland, Commissioners of National Education
An introduction to the art of reading, with suitable accent and intonation
    Dublin 1837. 2nd edition, Dublin 1844 (BL 08232.ee.10(3); NLI
8085.i.l). Further editions and reissues to at least 1869. The book's
principal aim is implied in its criticism of its predecessors: 'The usual
method of teaching Elocution has seldom had for its object the
rendering of the written language clear and perspicuous; but merely
the communicating of pleasing musical cadences'. Cf no. 50 above.

69 (1842) George Frederick Graham
*English; or, the art of composition explained in a series of instructions
and examples*
    1842 (BL); 2nd edition 1844; as *The art of English composition*,
1855. Interesting preface: 'I…think it very questionable whether general
disquisitions upon virtue or vice have any *practical* effect upon the
youthful mind'. Cf no. 53 above.

70 (1846) Frederic Rowton
*The debater: a new theory of the art of speaking; being a series of
complete debates, outlines of debates, and questions for discussion; with
references to the best sources of information on each particular topic*
    (Title from 2nd edition). 1846 (BL); 2nd edition revised 1850.
Another edition 1855. He complains that school teaching of elocution
produces 'a perfect reciter of other people's ideas' who 'cannot utter a
thought of his own'. Rowton's innovation is to practise discussion
rather than recitation.

71 (1866) Alexander Bain, 1818–1903, professor of English, Aberdeen
English composition and rhetoric, a manual
    1866. The work had four editions to 1877; in 1887/88 it was
substantially revised and enlarged, in two volumes. The revision
emphasized the analysis of the figures of speech as an aid to developing
a literary style. See below Harrington 1989.

72 (1868) John Hugh Hawley
*A complete course of English composition, in a series of familiar letters,
with numerous exercises; Oxford and Cambridge examination papers;
chapters on precis writing, etc*
    1868 (BL). A sequel to his *First course in English composition*, 1865.
A key to the exercises was published in 1869. Hawley says he was
'unconsciously' influenced by Bain, but his book is on much simpler lines.

A NEW

ENGLISH Accidence,

By way of Short

Queſtion and *Anſwer*,

Built upon the Plan of the *Latin Grammar*,
ſo far as it agrees with, and is conſiſtent with
the Nature and Genius of the ENGLISH
TONGUE.

Deſigned for the Uſe and Benefit, and Adapted to the

Capacity of YOUNG LADS

AT THE

ENGLISH SCHOOL.

In Order to teach them the Grounds of their
Mother Tongue, and fit them for the more
eaſy and expeditious attaining the *Grammar*
of the *Latin*, or any other *Language*.

By a SCHOOL-MASTER in the *Country*.

Humbly Addreſs'd to the Teachers of *Engliſh* Schools in *Great-*
Britain, and ſubmitted to their Candour and Judgment.

If no Children were to learn Latin, *or any other* Fo-
reign Language, 'till they had firſt learned the Art of
Grammar in their Mother *Tongue. I doubt not but our*
Latin *Schools, would ſoon become much more ſucceſsful*
and uſeful to the Nation, *than ever yet they have been*
Mr. *A. Lane's* Preface to his Art of Letters.

LONDON:

Printed for *James Hodges* at the *Looking-Glaſs* on *London-Bridge*,
and Sold by *H. Boad* and *J. Kendall*, Bookſellers at *Col-*
cheſter, and *W. Creighton*, Bookſeller in *Ipſwich*. 1736.

Title-page of *A new English accidence*, 1736

GRAMMAR AND LANGUAGE (G)

There is not much doubt as to whether a book is an English grammar. It may be meant more for adults than for school use; it may be part of a dictionary, a compendium, a spelling book, but it is obviously a grammar. Its contents, although varying in detail, are broadly uniform. This makes the very large number of grammars published since 1761 more surprising than is the corresponding number of literary works, which were varied and ambiguous. Other linguistic textbooks are easily identified. Dictionaries are included if they were explicitly intended for school use. During the hundred years after 1750 'exercises in false English' were a popular part of many textbooks (no. 86), and a number of books were published consisting of nothing else. The few textbooks of punctuation are represented here: their outlook is more often grammatical than rhetorical. During the nineteenth century the history of the language was increasingly taught, eventually in separate textbooks but usually within a grammar (no. 94), together with word-formation and etymology.

Throughout the whole period the grammars express both the dominance of Latin and the continuous efforts of a small number of teachers to escape from it. The books reflect also the expectation that pupils should memorise grammar rules, whether or not they understood them. The definition and function of the parts of speech were learnt by heart and applied in the exercise of parsing. Syntax was studied by memorising and applying perhaps twenty, or two hundred, rules. English was treated as a dead language until the influence of German philologists stimulated a latent interest in its history and in language itself. Such interest is apparent in a few textbooks from earlier times, but in scholarly works which made little general impact.

The grammars increase steadily in bulk as well as in number. During the seventeenth century it was often said that English, because it had few inflections, had little grammar. In the eighteenth century English was thought to have at least as much grammar as Latin. By the second half of the nineteenth century there were some teachers who wanted to raise the status of English as a subject by making its textbooks as bulky as Latin grammars, but more difficult.

73 (1633) Charles Butler, *c.*1560–1647, master of Basingstoke School
The English grammar, or the institution of letters, syllables and words,
in the English tongue. Whereunto is annexed an index of words like
and unlike
   Oxford 1633 (BL); another issue Oxford 1634 (BL). The 1634 issue
was edited by A. Eichler, Halle 1910. Butler is mostly interested in the
mildly reformed spelling system in which the book is printed. The
grammar is thin; there is no syntax.

74 (1700) A. Lane, dead by 1705, 'Late master of the Free School of
Leominister in Herefordshire, now teacher of a private school at
Mile-End-Green near Stepney'
A key to the art of letters, or English as a learned language, full of art,
elegancy and variety. Being an essay to enable both foreigners, and the
English youth of either sex, to speak and write the English tongue well
and learnedly, according to the exactest rules of grammar...With a
preface shewing the necessity of a vernacular grammar
   1700 (BL); 1705 (Bodley); 2nd edition 1706 (OUP); Scolar Press
facsimile of 1700 edition, 1969. The earliest attempt to write an English
grammar for schools which was suited to English rather than Latin; but
the changes are only in the arrangement of the parts of speech and in
some terminology. Preface full of interest.

75 (1711) James Greenwood, died 1737, usher to Benjamin Morland
at Hackney Academy; later Sur-master at St Paul's
An essay towards a practical English grammar. Describing the genius
and nature of the English tongue: giving likewise a rational and plain
account of grammar in general, with a familiar explanation of its terms
   1711 (BL); 2nd edition 1722 (BL); 3rd edition 1729 (BL; Nottingham
UL); two further editions to 1753; Scolar Press facsimile of 1711 edition,
1968. A comprehensive grammar, owing much to Wallis. Abridged as
The Royal English Grammar, 1737, and eight further editions to 1780.
Cf no. 30 above.

76 (1711) [Charles Gildon] 1655–1724, miscellaneous writer
A grammar of the English tongue, with notes, giving the grounds and
reason of grammar in general...Adapted to the use of schools
   1711 (BL; Bodley); 2nd edition adds *the arts of poetry, rhetoric, logic,*
&c. Making a compleat system of an English education, 1712 (BL); six
further editions to 1782; Scolar Press facsimile of 1711 edition, 1967.
The grammar was in some way sponsored by John Brightland; it was
also associated with Richard Steele and has been attributed to both,
incorrectly. The second edition is the principal one. The grammar
itself is derivative, but it was much quoted.

77   (1753) *A pocket dictionary or complete English expositor: shewing*
readily the part of speech to which each word belongs; its true meaning,
when not self-evident; its various senses, if more than one, placed in
proper order; and the language, from whence it is deriv'd, pointed out
immediately after the explication [etc]
    1753 (BL). Four editions in all to 1779. The title-page of 1753 is
reproduced in Alston 5, below. The dictionary is sometimes attributed
to its publisher, John Newbery. Cf no. 32 above.

78   (1754) James Gough, born 1712, master of a school at Cork, and his
brother John Gough, 1721–91, master of a school at Lisburn.
A practical grammar of the English tongue. Containing the most
material rules and observations for understanding the English
language well, and writing it with propriety
    Dublin 1754 (BL); eight editions in all to 1801. Scolar Press facsimile
of 1754 edition, 1967. A good example of a thoughtful, conventional
grammar.

79   (1761) Joseph Priestley, 1733–1804, sometime teacher
The rudiments of English grammar; adapted for the use of schools.
With observations on style
    1761 (BL). Pages 65–92 are 'Examples of English composition,'
ie prose and verse passages. At least ten further editions to 1826; also
reprinted in vol. 23 of his *Works*. J T. Rutt (ed.). Scolar Press facsimile
of 1761 edition, 1969. Priestley comments on 'the remarkable simplicity'
of English, and his grammar reflects such a view.

80   (1762) [Robert Lowth] 1710–87, Bishop of London
A short introduction to English grammar: with critical notes
    1762 (BL); 2nd edition revised 1763 (BL: Bodley); more than fifty
further British and American editions to 1838; Scolar Press facsimile
of 1762 edition, 1969. It combines a scholarly tone with simplicity
of presentation; very popular throughout the eighteenth century;
encouraged the practice of picking on incorrect usage among
contemporary writers. See below Pullum 1974.

81   (1777) H. Ward, 'School-master in Whitehaven'
A short, but clear system of English grammar, with exercises of bad
English, designed for the use of schools, and for those gentlemen and
ladies who may want the assistance of a master
    Whitehaven 1777 (Carlisle PL). 'Want' of course, means 'lack'.

82 (1788) William Chown 'Schoolmaster at Moulton, near Northampton'
English grammar epitomised: or, a short, plain, easy compendium of
English grammar, for the use of youth at schools
   Northampton [1788] (BL). A short work, which he says can be learnt
by heart in two months by a boy of 'tolerable common Capacity'. He
urges young people to read, 'even a common News-paper'.

83 (1794) Alexander Barrie 'Teacher of English'
A spelling and pronouncing dictionary of the English language, for the
use of schools...to which are added the principles of English grammar
   Edinburgh 1794 (BL). The final word in the dictionary is
anthropomorphitanianismicaliation.

84 (1795) Lindley Murray, 1745–1826
English grammar, adapted to the different classes of learners, with an
appendix, containing rules, and observations for promoting perspicuity
in speaking and writing
   York 1795. A thorough compilation of accepted practices, not without a personal point of view. It has been estimated that there were 200
editions worldwide before 1850, with copies in most libraries. He
wrote also an *Abridgment* of it, 1797; *Exercises* on it, 1797; *Key to the*
exercises, 1797. Cf no. 39 above. See below Pressly 1938; Read 1939;
Chilton 1954; Vorlat 1959; Jones 1983.

85 (1815) Joseph Sutcliffe
A grammar of the English language. To which is added, a series of
classical examples of the structure of sentences, and three important
systems of the time of verbs
   1815 (BL); 2nd edition 're-composed, and made into a new work',
1821 (BL). 'Time' here means 'tense'. The preface lists and discusses
some of the main grammars of the eighteenth century. The work has
a strong historical and comparative tone.

86 (1825) John Kigan
A practical English grammar, agreeably to the new system. Adapted to
the use of schools, and private students; containing copious examples
of wrong choice of words, under Etymology; and wrong arrangement
of them under Syntax. With a key
   Belfast 1825 (Cambridge UL; Bodley). The 'new system' is that put
forward in his *Remarks on the practice of grammarians*, 1823. The
main reform was a limitation to two parts of speech, noun and verb;
a minor reform was the introduction of the semi-comma.

87 (1832) Henry Young, of Spalding, Lincs
The youth's memoriter and English exercise book, in two parts;
containing a rational grammar of the English language...a verbal
analysis, or a method of acquiring the significations of words by a
knowledge of their component parts or elements; and orthographical
exercises, upon a plan entirely new...etc
   1832 (BL). An attempt to simplify English grammar by rejecting 'cases,
moods, compound tenses, and the numbers and persons of our verbs'.

88 (1834) John Murray McCulloch, headmaster, Circus-Place School,
Edinburgh
A manual of English grammar, philosophical and practical; with
exercises; adapted to the analytical mode of tuition. For the use of
schools, or of private students
   Edinburgh 1834 (BL); 24th edition 1873 (BL). Price 1s 6d in 1856.
His aim is to 'exhibit Grammar as a science'. It is the province of the
grammarian 'not to dictate what usages ought to be, but simply to
discover what they are.' Cf no. 46 above.

89 (1838) William Birkin, 'Master of an academy in Derby'
The rational English expositor, and guide to pronunciation; containing
an extensive selection of words, arranged on a new and systematic plan,
with copious and accurate definitions [etc]
   Derby 1838 (Hammersmith PL). Price 1s 6d. In spite of his claim
there is nothing new about the book; it is an etymologically inclined
spelling book.

90 (1841) Alexander Allen, 1814–42, headmaster, Madras House School,
Hackney, & James Cornwell, 1812–1902, principal, Borough Road
Training College
A new English grammar, with very copious exercises, and a systematic
view of the formation and derivation of words.
   1841 (BL); at least thirty-eight editions to 1866 and many
unnumbered ones to 1893. An influential grammar, introducing a
number of new features, described in the preface. 'A person who
does not understand grammar can scarce think correctly, for he
cannot speak correctly; and correct speaking generally accompanies
(logically) correct thinking'.

91 (1841) Benjamin Humphrey Smart, *c.*1786–1872, writer and
independent teacher of elocution.
The accidence and principles of English grammar
    1841 (BL); another edition 1847. Smart's independence was
intellectual as well as professional. He advocated the reintegration of
the subjects of the trivium, and wrote on all of them. His eighteen
works on language and linguistics are today receiving more attention
than they did in his lifetime. The grammar puts great stress on the
formation of words, especially prefixes and suffixes, and on historical
development. See below Esbach 1978.

92 (1841) Hugh Doherty
An introduction to English grammar, on universal principles
    1841 (BL). An idiosyncratic, but not trivial, attempt to make up for
the 'antiquated methods of schools…unintelligible to the majority of
students'. The difficulties in school are perpetuated by 'the private
interests of schoolmasters' in order to make 'their assistance absolutely
necessary. This is a natural consequence of incoherence in social
organization'.

93 (1843) George Crane
*The principles of language; exemplified in a practical English grammar.
With copious exercises. Designed as an introduction to the study of
languages generally, for the use of schools, and self instruction*
    1843 (BL). He taught abroad and was influenced by Becker. One of
the earliest advocates of clause analysis.

94 (1843) Robert Gordon Latham, 1812–88, professor of English,
University College, London
An elementary English grammar for the use of schools
    1843 (BL; Bodley). At least six further issues to 1875 (BL). He thinks
there are two levels of grammatical knowledge: that for everyday use
can be learnt by 'attending to the language of the best sort'; the higher
level is for 'knowing the history, or of reasoning on the principles of the
English language'. He wrote grammars for several types of school. See
below Quirk 1974.

95 (1851) William Manneville, 'Translator of languages, and teacher of
the classics and mathematics'
*English grammar simplified. Designed for the use of schools and
self-tuition*
    [1851] (BL). He shows an unusual knowledge of earlier grammars,
but relies chiefly on Crombie.

96 (1852) John Daniel Morell, 1816–91, inspector of schools
*The analysis of sentences explained and systematised. After the plan of
Becker's German Grammar*

  [1852] (BL). Eight further editions to 1858. The emphasis of the
book is on syntax, for which teachers have no common vocabulary.
His analytical approach, especially to clause analysis, was influential, in
this and in many other textbooks.

97 (1855) Thomas Goodwin 'Headmaster of the Greenwich Proprietary
School'
*The student's practical grammar of the English language; together with
a commentary on the first book of Milton's Paradise Lost: containing a
practical analysis thereof, critical and grammatical...Intended for use in
schools and adapted to meet the needs of self-instructing students*

  1855 (BL). He sees analysis as the most important aspect of the
changes in instruction during the last twenty years. A thorough mastery
of one book of Milton will fit you to understand 'any book in the
English language'.

98 (1858) Charles Peter Mason, 1820–1900, Fellow of University College,
London
English grammar

  1858 (BL); 2nd edition 1861 (BL); forty editions in all to 1901.
Much revised; much praised. He knows of 430 previous grammars
and estimates another 70 contemporary ones. The scholarly ones are
unsuited to school and those which are simple enough for school are
'defaced by serious inaccuracies and omissions'.

99 (1863) George Coutie, 'English master of Liverpool High School'
*Word expositor and spelling-guide: a school manual, exhibiting the
spelling, pronunciation, meaning, and derivation of all the important
and peculiar words in the English language. With copious exercises
for examination and dictation*

  1863 (BL); at least two editions to 1882. He puts forward as an
innovation his thematic arrangement of vocabulary, eg 'Words relating
to time...to the army...to commerce'.

100 (1864) Roscoe Mongan
*The practical English grammar; comprising also an analysis of
sentences; composition, &c.*

  1864 (Glasgow UL; BL). An ordinarily derivative work aimed at
public examinations. An abridgment was issued in the same year.

SAMPLE TEXTBOOKS: LISTED ALPHABETICALLY

RSP 1–27   RL 28–59   EX 60–72   G 73–100

90   Allen & Cornwell, *New English grammar* (1841)

20   *The Anti-spelling book* (1833)

59   Armstrong, *Compendium of English literature* (1870)

32   *Art of poetry made easy* (1746)

71   Bain, *English composition & rhetoric* (1866)

83   Barrie, *Spelling & pronouncing dictionary* (1794)

24   Bevan, *Reading without tears* (1857)

89   Birkin, *Rational English expositor* (1838)

51   Boyes, *English repetitions* (1848)

5   Browne, *English school reformed* (1700)

54   Buchan, *Poetical reader* (1859)

64   Burgh, *Art of speaking* (1761)

73   Butler, *English grammar* (1633)

19   Campbell, *Child's economic instructor* (1829)

9   *Child's new plaything* (1742)

22   *Child's treasure* (1851)

82   Chown, *English grammar epitomised* (1788)

12   Clarke, *Rational spelling book* (1772)

1   Clement, *Petie schoole* (1587)

15   Cook, *Westminster spelling book* (1791/2)

2   Coote, *English schoole-maister* (1596)

90   Cornwell (see Allen & Cornwell)

99   Coutie, *Word expositor* (1863)

60   Cox, *Art or crafte of rhethoryke* (c.1525)

93   Crane, *Principles of language* (1843)

SAMPLE TEXTBOOKS: LISTED CHRONOLOGICALLY BY NUMBER

RSP 1–27   RL 28–59   EX 60–72   G 73–100

*c.*1525	60	1772	12	1838	49
1576	1	1774	37	1841	90
1596	2	1777	81	1841	91
1597	28	1781	13	1841	92
		1783?	38	1842	69
1633	73	1788	82	1842	21
1640	3	1790	14	1843	93
1657	29	1792/3	15	1843	94
1672	61	1794	83	1845	50
1686	4	1795	84	1846	70
		1799	39	1848	51
1700	5			1849	52
1700	74	*c.*1800	65	1851	22
1711	75	1800	16	1851	95
1711	76	1801	17	1852	53
1712	6	1801	40	1852	96
1717	30	1801	66	1854	23
1719	7	1815	85	1855	97
1721	62	*a.*1816	67	1857	24
1737	31	1816	41	1858	98
1738	63	1818	42	1859	54
1740	8	1821	18	1860	55
1742	9	1822	43	1862	56
1746	32	1825	86	1863	99
1750	33	1827	44	1863	57
1753	77	*a.*1829	19	1863	58
*a.*1754	10	1831	45	1864	100
1754	78	1831	46	1866	71
1756	34	1832	87	1866	25
1761	64	1833	20	1866	26
1761	79	1834	88	1868	72
1761	35	1835	47	1869	27
1762	80	1835	48	1870	59
1762	36	1837	68		
1763	11	1838	89		

MODERN WORKS

There are as yet no historical studies of textbooks of English generally. Textbooks are necessarily prominent in the few historical surveys of English teaching (Shayer 1972; Michael 1987) but they are there treated as evidence for teaching methods, not as the principal objects of enquiry. There are some studies of individual books (Hornbeak 1934; Burness 1988) and of individual authors (Wallis 1954; Benzie 1972) but the bulk of the relevant literature is concerned with particular aspects of English teaching: grammar, especially, basic reading and class readers. In the United States there has been some detailed study of American literary texts, but limited to content analysis and some of the deductions which can be made from it. Earlier work, in several countries, on nationalistic bias in history and geography books has had good results. In mathematics and in the sciences work has concentrated on the identification of historically prominent books.

The study of textbooks, broadly conceived, is still only beginning. In 1903 Foster Watson, Professor of Education at Aberystwyth, complained: 'Nowhere that I know is to be found any account of the textbooks used in the schools, particularly in the provincial schools'. Apart from Watson's own work little has been done since to improve our knowledge. There has, however, been a vast extension of our bibliographical resources and of facsimile editions. The social significance of textbooks has yet to be systematically considered; their printing and publishing histories have yet to be investigated; the authors and their motivation are for the most part obscure.

It is difficult therefore to compile a satisfactory bibliography of modern works relating to the history of textbooks in English. A strictly relevant list would be unhelpfully short; but once the strictness is relaxed there are no clear limits to what might be useful: biography; letters; social and cultural history; journals such as *The Gentleman's Magazine* and *The Critical Review*; history of education; school histories; local histories; history of publishing houses and their archives; antiquarian booksellers' catalogues – all are possible sources of information.

The following list is inconsistently selective, and not all items have been examined. Suggestions will improve it. The dominance of linguistic studies reflects the imbalance of scholarship in this field. Grammar attracts, irrationally, the impetuous attention of historians, critics, journalists and politicians, whereas the textbook evidence for the teaching of literature and of expression is neglected. Most of the relevant bibliographies deal with a wider field than just English; they are to appear in a later book of this series, a guide to the study of textbooks generally. Purely American textbooks have also been left to a later book, except for one study (Monaghan 1983) which is included as a model for which there is no British equivalent. Some early twentieth century studies of seventeenth- and eighteenth-century spelling books have been omitted because they deal only with phonology.

Aarsleff, Hans (1967) *The study of language in England 1780–1860.*
Minneapolis: U. Minneapolis Press; London: Athlone Press. Reprinted
with new preface, 1983. Valuable background study.

Aarts, F.G.A.M. (1985) 'William Cobbett: radical reactionary and poor
man's grammarian', *Neophilologus* 70. Pp 603–14. Discusses also
grammars besides Cobbett's of 1818.

Aarts, F.G.A.M. (1948) 'English grammars and the Dutch contribution,
1891–1985', U. of Duisberg, Linguistic Agency, Series A, Paper 148.
He distinguishes scholarly grammars, dealing with syntax, from school
grammars dealing with word classes.

Abercrombie, David (1958) Introduction to the Augustan Reprint Society's
facsimile edition of G.W, *Magazine*, 1703. He discusses authorship and
G.W.'s proposals for spelling reform. *Magazine* (which is a book) is
reprinted by the Scolar Press, 1968.

Abercrombie, David (1948) 'Forgotten phoneticians', reprinted in his
Studies in phonetics and linguistics, 1965, chapter 6. First published in
The Transactions of the Philological Society, 1948. He discusses five
seventeenth- and eighteenth-century spelling reformers who wished to help
teachers.

Adams, J.R.R. (1987) *The printed word and the common man: popular
culture in Ulster 1700–1900.* Belfast: Queens U. Institute of Irish Studies.
Describes chapbook literature, home and school reading, book distribution.

Algeo, John (1985) 'The earliest English grammars', in M-J. Arn, &
H. Wirtjes, *Historical and editorial studies in medieval and early modern
English. For Johan Gerritson,* Groningen. He defends reliance on
traditional Latin grammatical categories.

Alston, R.C. [In progress] *A bibliography of the English language from the
invention of printing to the year 1800. I English grammars,* Leeds 1965.
IV Spelling books, Bradford 1967. *V The English dictionary,* Leeds 1966.
VI Rhetoric [etc], Bradford 1969. *X Education and language teaching,*
Leeds 1972. *Supplement,* Leeds 1973. Corrected reissue, 1974. An
essential work. Except in the first volume many title-pages and pages
of text are reproduced in facsimile.

Altick, Richard (1957) *The English common reader: a social history of the
mass reading public 1800–1900.* Chicago U. Press. Many later impressions.
Invaluable background, with some specific attention to textbooks.

Anders, H. (1936) 'The Elizabethan ABC with the catechism', *The Library* 4th series, 16. Pp 32–48. Reproduces surviving fragments; useful description of the relation between ABC and primer.

Axon, W.E.A. (1903) 'Hornbooks and ABCs'. Manchester, Lancs. & Cheshire Antiquarian Society *Transactions* 20. Reprinted 1903.

Bacon, W.A. (1964) 'The elocutionary career of Thomas Sheridan', *Speech Monographs* 31. Pp 1–53.

Baldwin, Thomas Whitfield (1944) *William Shakspere's petty school*. Urbana: Illinois U. Press. A rich but confusingly presented source of information about the ABC, the catechism, and doctrinal reading matter for young children.

Baldwin, Thomas Whitfield (1944) *William Shakspere's small Latine and lesse Greeke*. Urbana: Illinois U. Press. 2 vols. Substantial discussion of textbooks of rhetoric, but the bulk of the evidence is, naturally, Latin. Useful for the influence of Latin teaching on the writing of English.

Benzie, W. (1972) *The Dublin orator: Thomas Sheridan's influence on eighteenth century rhetoric and belles lettres*. Leeds U. School of English. Sheridan's books on elocution, aimed at teachers and older pupils in school, were influential in the teaching of literature.

Bergstrom, Folke (1955) 'John Kirkby (1746) on English pronunciation', *Studia Neophilologica* 27. Pp 65–104. Kirkby was at one time Gibbon's tutor and wrote *A new English grammar*, 1746.

Blunden, Edmund (1963) 'Elegant extracts', in *Essays on the eighteenth century presented to David Nichol Smith*. New York. Pp 225–237. First published in 1945. Reviews the contents of Vicesimus Knox's three influential anthologies. Cf no. 38 above.

Boggis, Doreen H. (1969) *Catalogue of the Hockliffe collection of early children's books*. Bedford College of Higher Education (xerox). For spelling books and readers and simple grammars.

Bolgar, R.R. (1983) 'The teaching of letter-writing in the sixteenth century', *Hist. Edn* 12. Pp 245–53. A good background to the multitudinous manuals, used in school, of the following centuries.

Bowen, John (1986) 'The subject of "English": psychology and pedagogy from Bain to Richards'. PhD dissertation, Birmingham U. Useful for Alexander Bain's textbooks of language and literature. Cf no. 71.

Bradshaw, Henry (1889) 'On the ABC as an authorised schoolbook in the sixteenth century', in *Collected papers of Henry Bradshaw*. CUP. Pp 333–40. Describes four ABCs of *c.*1538, *c.*1547, 1553 and 1631.

Breeze, Andrew (1988) 'Leonard Cox, a Welsh humanist in Poland and Hungary', *Nat. Lib. Wales J*, 25. Pp 399–410. Cox was headmaster of two grammar schools in Hungary and professor of literature at Cracow before becoming master of Reading School. Cf no. 60.

Burchfield, Robert (1991) 'The Fowler brothers and the tradition of usage handbooks', in G.Leitner (1991) below, pp. 93–111. Although strictly not textbooks *The King's English*, 1906, and *A dictionary of modern English usage*, 1926, were influential at every educational level.

Burness, Edwina (1988) 'Thomas Dawks's The Complete Englishman, (1685). A newly discovered seventeenth century dictionary', *English Studies* 69. Pp 331–40. Dawks's work is a spelling book, whose lists form a dictionary of an unusual kind.

Butterworth, Charles C. (1949) 'Early primers for the use of children', *Papers of the Bibliographical Society of America* 43. Pp 374–82. Background discussion of identification and dating.

Butterworth, Charles C. (1953) *The English primers (1529–1545): their publication and connection with the English Bible and the Reformation in England*. Philadelphia: U. Pennsylvania Press. The primers are relevant because they were regularly the first reading matter after the ABC.

C, R.W. & P,W.G. (1928) 'The Golden Treasury, its bibliographical adventures; the varying issues of the first edition', *Bookman's Journal* 16.5. Pp 268–76. Palgrave's anthology was first published in 1861.

Cannon, Garland H. (1979) 'English grammars of the seventeenth and eighteenth centuries', *Semiotica* 26. Pp 121–49.

Carpenter, Humphrey & Prichard, Mari (1984) *The Oxford companion to children's literature*. OUP. Valuable for the many works which might be read either in school or at home.

Case, Arthur E. (1935) *A bibliography of English poetical miscellanies, 1521–1750*. Bibliographical Society.

Chalmers, George S. (1976) *Reading easy, 1800–1850*. London: Broadsheet King. A valuable survey full of tantalising omissions. Contains more than fifty facsimile pages from early reading and spelling books.

Chilton, C.W. (1954) 'Lindley Murray, a forgotten figure'. U. Hull Institute Edn, *Studies in Education* 2. Pp 144–50. Not so forgotten now. Cf nos 39 and 84, above.

Cohen, Murray (1977) *Sensible words. Linguistic practice in England, 1640–1785.* Baltimore: Johns Hopkins Press. Valuable: Cohen judges eighteenth-century English grammars on their own terms and accepts them as useful evidence in the study of linguistic and cultural history.

Constantinescu, Ilrica (1974) 'John Wallis, 1616–1703. A reappraisal of his contribution to the study of English', *Historiographica Linguistica* 1. Pp 297-311. Wallis wrote, in Latin, an influential grammar of English, *Grammatica Linguae Anglicanae*, 1653, the fifth edition of which was reprinted and translated by John Kemp in 1972 (Longman).

Dallas R.C. (1809) 'Biographical memoirs of James Elphinston'. *Gentleman's Magazine* 79.2. Pp 1057–63. Elphinston wrote works on spelling reform and an English grammar, and compiled a verse anthology for schools.

Darton, F.J. Harvey (1982) *Children's books in England.* CUP, 3rd edition. First published in 1932. Takes particular account of the educational aspects of children's literature.

Davies, Frank (1973) *Teaching reading in early England.* Pitman. Describes methods of teaching reading from ancient times to 1612. Chapter 5 discusses basic reading material: hornbook, primer, psalter, catechism. Not entirely reliable.

Dobson, E.J. (1968) *English pronunciation, 1500–1700,* 2nd edition. 2 vols. OUP. First published 1957. For books on spelling and pronunciation. Very full discussion, necessarily from a phonological point of view.

Downey, Charlotte (1991) 'Factors in the growth of the English language in 18th and 19th century Ireland', in G. Leitner (1986), pp 81–91. Refers to several eighteenth-century grammars.

Ellis, Alec (1971) *Books in Victorian elementary schools.* Library Association. Describes the extent to which the Bible, rather than secular books, was used to teach reading.

Enkvist, N.E. (1975) 'English in Latin guise: a note on some renaissance textbooks', *Historiographica Linguistica* 2. Pp. 283–98.

Eschbach, Achim (1978) *Benjamin Humphrey Smart: Grundlagen der Zeichentheorie: grammatik, logik, rhetorik.* Frankfurt-am-Main: Syndikat.

Evans, B.I. (1932) 'Tennyson and the origins of the Golden Treasury', *Times Literary Supplement,* 8 Dec. An account, based on Palgrave's manuscript in the British Library, of the compilation of the anthology and of Tennyson's influence on it.

Ford, Paul Leicester (1897) *The New England Primer: a history of its origin
...with a reprint of the unique copy of the earliest known edition (1727).*
New York: Columbia Univ. Teachers College. Reissued in 1962. Discusses
the relation between *The New England Primer* and Benjamin Harris's *The
Protestant Tutor*, *a*.1686, and his *The New English Tutor*, *c*.1714, both
published in London.

Funke, Otto (1934) *Englische Sprachphilosophie im spaeteren 18
Jahrhundert,* Bern. Dated, but still useful for Harris and Horne Tooke,
who both influenced writers of school grammars.

Funke, Otto (1940) 'Ben Jonson's English Grammar (1640)', *Anglia* 64.
Pp 117–34. Describes Johnson's dependence on Ramus. See also Herford
& Simpson, below.

Funke, Otto (1941) *Die Fruehzeit der englische Grammatik...von Bullokar
bis Wallis.* Bern: Schriften der literarischen Gesellschaft, no. 41. Discusses
the background to the earliest grammars of English.

Giles, E.L. (1938) 'John Newton on education', *Notes & Queries* 175.
Pp 22–24. Recognises Newton's importance but considers, and quotes
from, his *School Pastime*, 1669, only. Newton wrote a number of textbooks for schools, including logic, rhetoric and grammar.

Goldsmith, P.L. (1980) 'Education for the nation and the individual: the
works of Vicesimus Knox II of Tonbridge, 1752–1821'. Ph D dissertation.
U. Western Australia. There is a copy in Tonbridge School Library.

Goldstrom, J.M. (1972) *The social content of education, 1808–70. A study
of the working-class school reader in England and Ireland.* Shannon: Irish
U. Press. An important study, with useful references.

Haass, Sabine (1985) 'Victorian poetry anthologies: their role and success in
the nineteenth century book market', *Publishing History* 17. Pp 51–64.

Hansen, Volker (1987) 'Vicesimus Knox: the teaching of English literature
for the liberalization of the mind', *Hist. Edn Soc. Bulletin* 39. Pp 19–23.

Harrington, Brian (1989) 'Alexander Bain: a reappraisal', *Hist. Edn Soc.
Bulletin* 44. Pp 46–51. Questions the value and interest of Bain's English
textbooks.

Heath, Shirley Brice (1989) 'Talking the text in teaching composition', in
S. De Castell, A. Luke and C. Luke, *Language, authority and criticism.*
London: Falmer. Pp 109–122. Contains some historical references.

Herford, C.H, Simpson, Percy & Evelyn (1947, 1952) *Ben Jonson's Works,*
III (for the text of his *English Grammar*); XI (for a commentary on it).

Higson, C.W.J. (1967) Supplement 1976, *Sources for the history of education.* Library Association.

Hornbeak, Katherine Gee (1934) *The Complete Letter Writer in English 1568–1800.* Smith Studies in Modern Languages 15, nos 3 & 4. Northampton, Mass.

Horner, Peter (1984) 'The development of reading books in England from 1870', in Greg Brooks and A.K. Pugh , *Studies in the History of Reading.* Centre for the Teaching of Reading, U. of Reading. Pp 80–84. A slight but useful overview.

Howell, Wilbur S. (1971) *Eighteenth century British logic and rhetoric.* Princeton U. Press. Essential source and descriptive material.

Howell, Wilbur S (1956) *Logic and rhetoric in England, 1500–1700.* Princeton U. Press. 2nd edition 1961. Howell's work on rhetoric has been adversely criticized by Vickers, below.

Johnson, Clifton (1904) *Old-time schools and school-books.* New York. Reprinted with new introduction, Dover Books 1963. Includes a description of British spelling books used in America, but is mainly concerned with American spelling books, readers and grammars before 1830. Illustrated.

Jones, Bernard (1983) 'William Barnes on Lindley Murray's English Grammar', *English Studies* 64. Pp 30–35. Discusses Murray's grammar and Barnes's objections to Murray's treatment of case and tense.

Jones, M.G. (1938) *The charity school movement.* CUP. Reprinted by Cass 1964. Pp 373–75 contain a list of eighteenth century books recommended for teachers and children.

Jones Stanley (1987) 'The suppression of Hazlitt's New and Improved Grammar of the English Tongue', *The Library* (6th series) 9. Pp 32–43.

Kearney, Anthony (1980) 'J.W. Hales and the teaching of English literature, 1860–1900', *Hist. Edn Soc. Bulletin* 26. Pp 42–46. Hales edited several English textbooks, notably *Longer English Poems,* 1872.

Kennedy, Arthur Garfield (1927) *A bibliography of writings on the English language...to the end of 1922.* Reprinted 1961. Entries before 1800 have been superseded by Alston (above).

Kinnell, Margaret, (1988) '"Sceptreless, free, uncircumscribed", radicalism, dissent and early children's books'. *British J. Edl. Studies* 36. Pp 49–71. For educational children's books, Sir Richard Phillips and the Godwins.

Kittredge, George Lynam (1906) *Some landmarks in the history of English grammar, with illustrations from the collection of George Plimpton.* Reissued, with one less illustration, as *English grammars of five centuries.* Boston, Mass. 1911.

Law, Alexander (1965) *Education in Edinburgh in the 18th century.* U. London Press. Chapter 6 includes a section on textbooks of English.

Law, Alexander (1984) 'Scottish schoolbooks of the eighteenth and nineteenth centuries', *Studies in Scottish Literature* 19. Pp 56–71. Briefly describes anthologies ('collections') and early reading books published by Chambers and Nelson.

Leitner, Gerhard (1986a) 'English grammars – past, present and future', in G. Leitner, *The English Reference Grammar*, Tübingen. Pp 409–31. Emphasizes the sociological aspects of the production of school grammars.

Leitner, Gerhard (1986b) 'English traditional grammars in the nineteenth century', in D. Kastowski and A. Swedzek, *Linguistics across historical and geographical boundaries.* 2 vols. Berlin, 2. Pp 1333–35.

Lufford, M. (1972) 'The provision of poetry for children in England from the seventeenth century to the present day'. MA dissertation, U. Sheffield.

M'Alester, Charles J. (1961) *A sketch of the life and literary labours of the late Robert Sullivan.* Belfast. Sullivan wrote several textbooks, including no. 21 above.

McDunphy, T.A. (1976) 'Christian Brothers in print', *Christian Brothers Educational Record.* Rome. Pp 129–46. An account of the textbooks and manuals published by the Congregation, including English readers and grammars from 1843 to 1967.

Marshall, J.J. (1908) 'David Manson, schoolmaster in Belfast'. *Ulster J. Archaeology*, Series 2, 14. Pp 59–72. Manson was an innovative teacher who wrote *A new primer*, c.1757, and *A new pocket dictionary*, 1762.

Mathieson, Margaret (1975) *The preachers of culture.* Allen & Unwin. Incidental mention of late nineteenth- and twentieth-century textbooks.

Michael, Ian (1988) 'Early teachers of reading: their struggles and methods from the sixteenth century', in C. Anderson (ed.) *Reading: the ABC and beyond.* Macmillan for United Kingdom Reading Association. Pp 226–236. Quotes from many early spelling and reading books.

Michael, Ian (1970) *English grammatical categories and the tradition to 1800.* CUP. A study based on practically all the English grammars published before 1801.

Michael, Ian (1987) *The teaching of English from the sixteenth century to 1870.* CUP. The bibliography lists more than 2,000 textbooks. Modesty and honesty are in conflict in describing this as currently the standard work.

Michael, Ian (1991) 'More than enough English grammars', in G. Leitner (ed.) *English traditional grammars: an international perspective.* Amsterdam: Benjamins. Pp 11–26.

Michael, Ian (forthcoming) 'Teaching literature: the historical background' in A. Light, R. Samuel and S. Regan (eds), *The idea of English, past and present.* CUP for History Workshop.

Monaghan, E. Jennifer (1983) *A common heritage: Noah Webster's Blue-back Speller.* Hamden, Connecticut: Archon Books. A model study of a particular textbook.

Moon, Marjorie (1976) Supplement 1983; *John Harris's books for youth, 1801–1843. A check list.* Cambridge: Five Owls Press. Harris continued John Newbery's publishing business, and its spirit.

Murphy, James J. (1981) *Renaissance rhetoric. A short-title catalogue of works on rhetorical theory from the beginning of printing to AD 1700.* New York. Works in English are separately listed.

National Book League (1946) *Children's books of yesterday.* Catalogue of an exhibition arranged by Percy Muir. It lists recreational and instructional works, some ABCs, spelling books and grammars.

National Book League (1949) *The English at School.* Catalogue of an exhibition arranged by Arnold Muirhead, including textbooks from the sixteenth to the nineteenth centuries.

New Cambridge Bibliography of English Literature. George Watson (ed.), 1969–77. Replaces *The Cambridge Bibliography of English Literature,* but both need to be consulted for textbooks.

Noblett, W. (1972) 'John Newbery: publisher extraordinary', *Hist. Today* 22. Pp 265–71. Cf no. 32, above.

Osborne: *The Osborne collection of early children's books, 1566–1910.* Vol. 1, ed. Judith St John, corrected reprint, Toronto 1975; first published in 1958. Vol. 2, ed. Judith St John, Toronto 1975. Includes some textbooks and some of indeterminate status.

Padley, G.A. (1985) *Grammatical theory in western Europe, 1500–1700. The trends in vernacular grammar, 1.* CUP. Discusses English grammars of the period in a European context.

Poldauf, Ivan (1948) *On the history of some problems of English grammar before 1800*. Prague Studies in English. Prague: Charles U. Faculty of Philosophy. A pioneering work still valuable in spite of its wartime limitations.

Pressly, I. P. (1938) 'Lindley Murray, the grammarian', in A.Brown, *A York Miscellany*.

Pullum, G.K. (1974) 'Lowth's Grammar: a re-evaluation', *Linguistics* 137. Pp 63–78.

Quirk, Randolph (1974) 'The study of the mother tongue', *The Linguist and the English Language*. An account of R.G. Latham's work, delivered as an inaugural lecture, 1961. Cf no. 94 above.

Radencich, Marguerite C. (1988) 'An historical overview: the influence of early textbooks on the teaching of reading and spelling', *Spelling Progress Quarterly* 4. Pp 9–15.

Read, Allen Walker (1939) 'The motivation of Lindley Murray's grammatical work'. JEPG 38. Pp 525–39. Murray's grammar, no. 84 above, described in relation to his life.

Robertson, Jean (1942) *The art of letter writing. An essay on the handbooks published in England during the sixteenth and seventeenth centuries*. Liverpool. Includes a bibliography of the *Complete Letter Writer*, *1568–1700*.

Robins, Robert Henry (1985) 'The evolution of English grammar books since the renaissance', in G.Leitner (ed.) *The English Reference Grammar*. Tübingen. Pp 292–306.

Roscoe, Sidney (1973) *John Newbery and his successors, 1740–1810. A bibliography*. Wormley: Five Owls Press. An important work, listing elementary textbooks as well as children's books published by Newbery, who probably wrote some of them himself. Cf no. 32 above.

Rosenbach, A.S.W. (1933) *Early American children's books*, Portland, Maine. Reissued 1971 by Dover Books. An account of the author's collection, now housed in the Free Library, Philadelphia. Illustrated; full of information about instructional and recreational books from 1682 to 1836, including many first published in Britain.

Scheurweghs, G. & Vorlat, E. (1959) 'Problems of the history of English grammars', *English Studies* 60. Pp 135–43. Concerned particularly with the grammars of Greaves 1594, Gildon 1711 and Ash 1760.

Scruton, William (1895) 'Joseph Hinchcliffe, schoolmaster'. *Bradford Antiquary* 2. Pp 180–84. Hinchcliffe, author of *Dictates*, 1826 and *The Juvenile speaker*, 1829, ran a school in Bradford.

Shayer, David (1972) *The teaching of English in schools, 1900–1970.* Routledge. Substantial discussion of specific textbooks but no general consideration of them.

Skeat, Walter William (1888) 'English grammars', *Notes and Queries*, series 7, 6. Pp 120–2; 243–4; 302–3. A historical list, with many omissions, started by Sir Frederic Madden from booksellers' catalogues. Reprinted in Skeat's *Student's Pastime*, 1896. Pp 241–51.

Spufford, Margaret (1981) *Small books and pleasant histories. Popular fiction and its readership in seventeenth century England.* Methuen. Important because it deals with books which were not textbooks.

Stewart, W. (1952) 'English courses for schools, an examination of some grammar-school textbooks', *Educational Review* 4. Pp 207–18. Examines a type of school-book now disused.

Stockham, Peter (1974) *Chapbook abcs.* New York: Dover. Facsimile reprints of five nineteenth century pictorial ABCs.

Tieken-Boon van Ostade, Ingrid (1992) 'John Kirkby and "The Practice of speaking and writing English": identification of a manuscript', *Leeds Studies in English*, new series 23. Leeds: U. Leeds School of English. The manuscript is shown to be in the hand of John Kirkby and an earlier version of his *New English Grammar*, 1746.

Tilleard, James (1859) 'On elementary school books', *Transactions of the National Association for the Promotion of Social Science*. Pp 387–96. Reprinted as a separate publication in 1860 (12 pages). Discusses the number of books in various categories and the number of copies in each category ordered through the Committee of Council, 1856–59.

Tucker, Susie (1961) *English examined.* CUP. A collection of extracts, containing many from linguistic textbooks.

Tuer, Andrew White (1896) *History of the Horn-book.* 2 vols. London. 2nd edition London 1897; reissued New York: Bloom 1968. 1st edition reprinted 2 vols, Amsterdam 1971; 2nd edition reprinted 1 vol., New York: Arno Press 1979. All editions illustrated.

Turner, J.R. (1980) *William Bullokar's Pamphlet for Grammar, 1586.*
Vol. 2 of *The Works of William Bullokar.* Leeds Texts and Monographs,
new series 1. U. Leeds School of English. An edited facsimile of both the
two surviving copies of the grammar, each annotated by Bullokar.
Biographical information about Bullokar is given in vol.1 by B. Danielsson
and R.C. Alston 1966.

Vallins, G.H. (1957) *The Wesleys and the English language. Four essays.*
Epworth Press. Pp 9–25 deal with John Wesley's *English grammar.*

Vickers, Brian (1988) *In defence of rhetoric.* CUP. A historical survey,
strongest on classical and medieval texts. Useful bibliography.

Vorlat, Emma (1975) *The development of English grammatical theory,
1586–1737. With special reference to the parts of speech.* Louvain U.
Press. About twenty-five grammars of English are included in this thematic
survey.

Vorlat, Emma (1959) 'The sources of Lindley Murray's "The English
Grammar"', in *Leuvense Bijdragen* 48. Pp 108–25. An analysis of the
similarities between Murray's grammar and five earlier ones.

Wallis, P.J. (1954) 'Jos(h)ua Poole, schoolmaster', *Notes and Queries.*
Pp 386–87. A brief note about the little biographical information there is.
Poole wrote two English textbooks in addition to no. 29 above.

Wallis, P.J. (1955) 'Charles Hoole, 1609–67', U. Leeds Institute Education
Researches and Studies in Education, no. 11, pp 75–84. Hoole's *A New
Discovery of the old Art of Teaching Schoole,* 1660 (Scolar Press facsimile
1969) is an essential background text.

Watson, Foster (1903) 'The curriculum and textbooks of English schools
in the first half of the seventeenth century', *Transactions of the
Bibliographical Soc.* 6, pp 159–267. An expanded version of a paper
given in 1902, and a preliminary study for the following.

Watson, Foster (1908) *The English grammar schools to 1660: their
curriculum and practice.* CUP. Reprinted, Cass 1968. Some reference
to spelling books, but more important for its picture of the relation
between Latin and English.

Watson, Foster (1909) *The beginnings of the teaching of modern subjects
in English.* Pitman. Reprinted, Wakefield: S.R. Publishers 1971. Still an
important source for sixteenth-and seventeenth-century textbooks and
their place in the curriculum.

Weedon, Margaret (1982) 'Northanger Abbey', A letter in the *Times Literary Supplement*, 26 November, showing that Thomas Dyche's *A guide to the English Tongue* (first published in 1707 and many times subsequently) was the ultimate source of a quotation in Northanger Abbey. A rare piece of firm evidence (and then only indirect) of the influence of a textbook.

Wells, Christopher J. (1989) 'Edward Young's Complete English Scholar', *Henry Sweet Soc. Newsletter* 13, pp 8–12. Description of a recently discovered copy of the ninth edition of a spelling book first published in 1765.

Whalley, Joyce I. (1974) *Cobwebs to catch flies: illustrated books for the nursery and schoolroom, 1700–1900*. Elek. Includes illustrated grammars, spelling books and readers.

Whitehead, Winifred (1954) 'Poetry anthologies for the grammar school', *Use of English* 5, pp 168–73. Lists and comments on works in use in the 1950s.

Wright, Louis B (1935) *Middle-class culture in Elizabethan England*. N. Carolina U. Press. Reissued, Cornell U.P. for Folger Shakespeare Library 1958. Important for the study of informal reading resources.